Properties of Materials

Stiff or Bendable

Charlotte Guillain

Heinemann Library
Chicago, Illinois

www.heinemannraintree.com
Visit our website to find out
more information about
Heinemann-Raintree books.

To order:

☎ Phone 888-454-2279
💻 Visit www.heinemannraintree.com
    to browse our catalog and order online.

© 2009 Heinemann Library
an imprint of Capstone Global Library, LLC
Chicago, Illinois

Customer Service: 888-454-2279

Visit our website at www.heinemannraintree.com

Designed by Joanna Hinton-Malivoire
Photo research by Elizabeth Alexander
Printed and bound by South China Printing Company Ltd

13 12 11 10 09
10 9 8 7 6 5 4 3 2 1

Library of Congress Cataloging-in-Publication Data

Guillain, Charlotte.
  Stiff or bendable / Charlotte Guillain.
     p. cm. -- (Properties of materials)
  Includes bibliographical references and index.
  ISBN 978-1-4329-3291-6 (hc) -- ISBN 978-1-4329-3299-2
(pb) 1. Elasticity--Juvenile literature. 2. Bendable structures--
Juvenile literature. I. Title.
  TA418.G85 2008
  620.1′1232--dc22
                    2008055127

Acknowledgments
The author and publishers are grateful to the following for
permission to reproduce copyright material: Alamy pp. **15** (©
Geri Lavrov), **20** (© Helene Rogers), **23 bottom** (© Geri Lavrov);
© Capstone Publishers p. **22** (Karon Dubke); Corbis p. **21**
(© Reuters); Getty Images pp. **11** (Jae Rew/Riser), **17** (Penny
Tweedie), **18** (Carl D. Walsh/Aurora); iStockphoto p. **13**;
Photolibrary pp. **4**, **23 middle bottom** (Inaki Antonana/age
footstock), **5** (Pomerantz Rich/Botanica), **7** (Image Source), **14**
(Pierre Bourrier); Shutterstock pp. **6** (© Tomasz Parys), **8** (© Peter
Baxter), **9** (© Emin Ozkan), **10**, **23 top** (© Monkey Business
Images), **12**, **23** middle top (© Istvan Csak), **16** (© Stephen Aaron
Rees), **19** (© Rannev).

Cover photograph of a garden hose reproduced with permission
of Photolibrary (Digital Vision/Thomas Barwick). Back cover
photograph of someone folding paper reproduced with
permission of Shutterstock (© Rannev).

The publishers would like to thank Nancy Harris and Adriana
Scalise for their assistance in the preparation of this book.

Every effort has been made to contact copyright holders of
any material reproduced in this book. Any omissions will
be rectified in subsequent printings if notice is given to
the publisher.

Contents

Stiff Materials

Some things are stiff.

Stiff things can be hard.

Stiff things cannot bend.

Stiff things cannot stretch.

Bendable Materials

Some things are bendable.

Bendable things can be hard or soft.

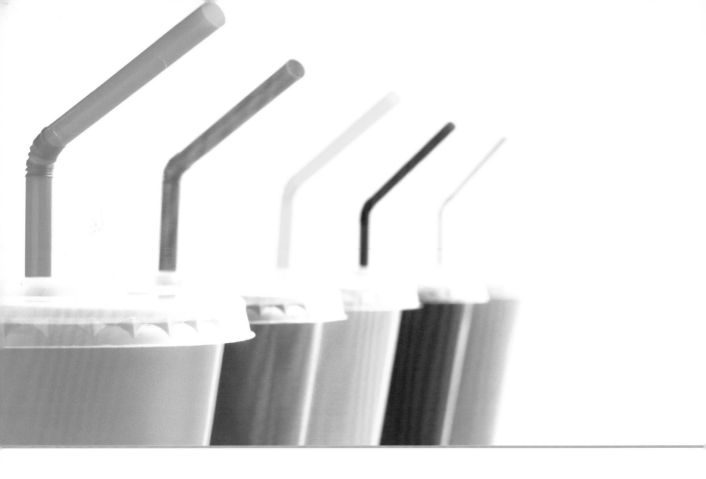

Bendable things can bend.

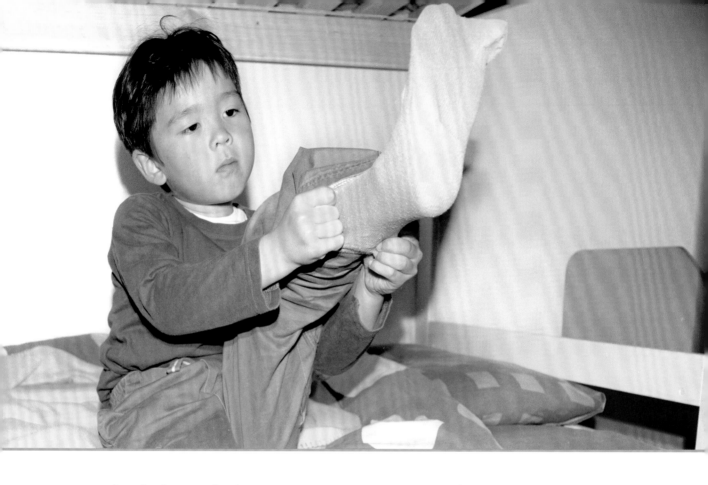

Bendable things can stretch.

Stiff and Bendable Materials

Plastic can be stiff.

You cannot bend stiff plastic.

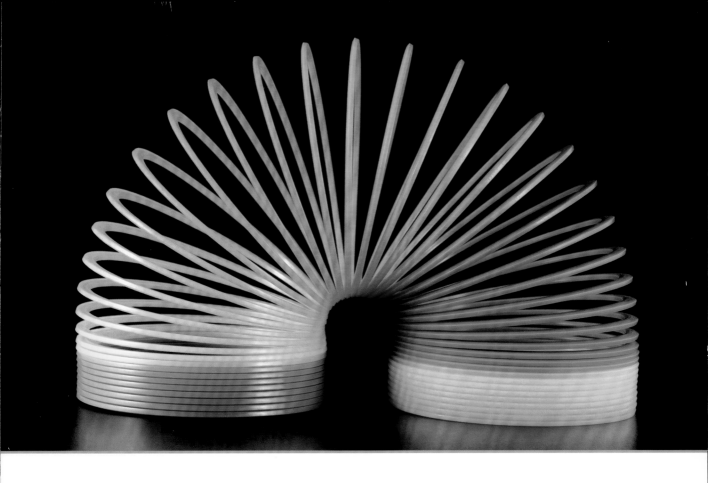

Plastic can be bendable.

You can bend bendable plastic.

Glass is stiff.

You cannot stretch it.

Rubber is bendable.
You can stretch it.

Wood is stiff.

You cannot stretch it.

Wool is bendable.
You can stretch it.

You can tell if something is stiff or bendable.

You can feel if something is stiff or bendable.

You can see if something is stiff
or bendable.

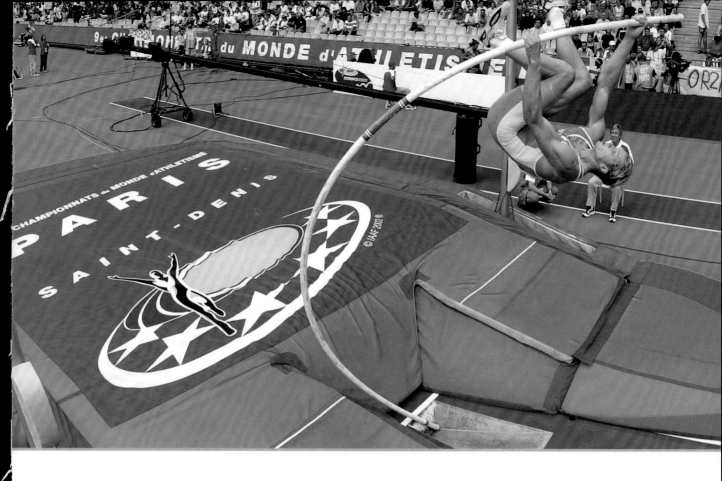

We can see when things are stiff.

We can see when things are bendable.

Quiz

Which of these things are stiff?

Which of these things are bendable?

Picture Glossary

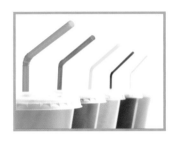
bendable material that can bend without breaking

plastic material that can be soft or hard

stiff hard to bend or move

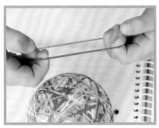
stretch to make something longer or wider, especially by pulling

Index

Note to Parents and Teachers
Before Reading
Tell children that materials can be stiff or bendable. Ask children if they know what the words "stiff" and "bendable" mean. Pass around several objects and have children guess if they are stiff or bendable. Possible objects to pass around are paper, a pencil, a spoon, a scarf, blocks, a straw, a glass cup, and a plastic cup.

After Reading
Have children make an object out of self-hardening clay. Mix 4 cups of flour and 1 cup of salt in a bowl. Add 1 cup of water gradually to form a ball. Knead until it no longer falls apart. Let children sculpt their clay. As they are molding their objects, ask children if the clay is bendable or stiff. Let their projects sit for a couple of days. After they harden, ask the children if they are bendable or stiff. Once the clay has completely hardened, help the children paint their projects!